GROW YOUR GLOW SERIES: BOOK I

GROW YOUR GLOW WITH
ROOT CHAKRA ENERGY

How to Utilize Root Chakra Energy to actively
manifest the Mind/Body Connection

LISA ANN REDA

DEDICATION

To God, the Universe, my Gatekeeper, Clara (who is my Mother-in-Law I never met on this physical Earth), all of my Spirit Guides and Angels and my Plant and Tree Spirits who continue to inspire me every day.

Never Let Age Be Your Cage and keep working on those Dream Boards!

TABLE OF CONTENTS

INTRODUCTION

It was like any other day, when I walked into the yoga workshop and met my fellow yoga enthusiasts, ready to take on the next three hours with vigor and open minds. The top floor room was warm, with many yoga implements neatly stacked in rows at the back. The wooden floor felt smooth and comforting beneath my bare feet as I walked across, feeling and hearing familiar creaks with every step.

As I unrolled my mat next to my neighbor, I carefully set my water bottle on one end of the mat, with my strap and wooden blocks close by. This was one of many workshops I explored at the *New Age Center* in downtown Nyack, New York back in 1994. I was only about 22 years old and I felt like I was destined to be there for these informative gatherings, with welcoming teachers, ready to educate me in various yoga poses and breathwork techniques.

What made this particular workshop stand out from the rest, was the experience I witnessed, firsthand. This led me to explore more about what is known as Chakras or energy centers found in areas along the spine in my body. Although I can't recall the exact workshop outline, I was left with a vivid memory that is responsible for my pursuit to learn more about this field over the coming years. The yoga teacher took us into a guided meditation emphasizing the Root Chakra, of which I was only then becoming aware of.

I cannot recall what was said by the instructor, but I do remember feeling this strong, hot energy that activated at the base of my spine. I was strangely and positively aware that this was the energy she was explaining. I was truly experiencing it at that moment. I brought my right hand to the base of my spine but I couldn't feel any heat on the outside of my skin. The feeling was internal, it was real, and this was a time I felt such a strong sense of a power ignited within me. From that day forward I have been able to activate it just by focusing and knowing that it is there.

Why does it have to be, that Chakras, or energy centers always seem to be mystical terms? Why not incorporate these extraordinary, meaning based, ethereal, aura motivating, glowing energies into every-day life? It's amazing how I did embrace yoga over the years, applied principles all along, and reaped the unique qualities that were brought out into my every-day life. You can do this, too and you can start today!

Once the awareness is conceived and the tools applied, you will realize that you can take this knowledge wherever you go. The goal is to try to resonate with your particular rainbow. Rainbow, in this book series, means the entire sequence of energy centers, starting from the base of the spine and continuing upward along the spinal column all the way to the top of the head. It refers to Red or Root Chakra, Orange or Sacral Chakra, Yellow or Solar Plexus Chakra, Green or Heart Chakra, Blue or Throat Chakra, Purple or Third Eye Chakra and White or Crown Chakra. Each Chakra will be a separate book in my Grow Your Glow Series because I feel there is so much information to process about each chakra that it would be easier to follow along book by book. Feel free to use them independently when they all become available. Mix and match as you see fit intuitively. This is about *your* life and how you can re-create it positively!

Before we go down the road in exploring the Root Chakra Energy, I would like to introduce the concept of Nutrition Intuition. This phrase will help you to remember the formula for using this book and any other books forthcoming in my Grow Your Glow Series.

Nutrition is the term which refers to mindfulness using Food and Fitness. Food meaning certain natural foods that are grown from the earth. In this book, I will explain how to incorporate mindfulness with certain foods, related to the Root Chakra which will enhance the qualities of the energy center into your daily life. I feel this is an extremely powerful and important category of Nutrition. Nutrition, in this book, will also refer to Fitness. Fitness which will refer to specific exercises that can work well with visualizing the Root center while doing the exercise and creating that more interesting aspect of mindfulness and laser focus, instead of just counting reps or pedaling into oblivion. Keep in mind, that the Nutrition Concept is associated with the first three chakras, Root,

Sacral and Solar Plexus Chakras which relate to the physical body and its workings.

Intuition, on the other hand, relates to the upper four chakras: Heart, Throat, Third Eye and Crown. These energy centers help develop mental and spiritual qualities within you. I will help you map out the particular techniques and exercises to enhance each of these chakras which will bring a new perspective to your life and how you connect to the Universe around you.

Meditation is a way to use your brain to clean the clutter of mind chatter while accessing up to 5% more of your brain which comes with bonuses that you already have. A quote I like to say, is: "Meditation is your brain on vacation". When do we ever really let our brain truly rest? Here, I will spell out how you can utilize the Rainbow in your beginner meditation, to restore your brain and get on the road to create your amazing new life.

So, take a journey with me into the awareness of Root Chakra and feel your life change. These principles are designed so you can recreate your daily life. You can retrain your mind and live with purpose every day. People will notice a change in you. You will gain confidence, creativity, calmness, and you will work that Root Chakra, to Resonate for you, and make your own path a reality!

Are you ready to learn how you can use Root Chakra Energy to start your practice of mindfulness? We must learn to walk before we can run. I will lead you down the first steps of the path with Root Chakra. Together, we will learn about the qualities of the Root Chakra and how to develop mindfulness through four important tools.

Chapter 1

What is a Chakra?

What is a chakra? A chakra is a wheel of spinning energy. Chakras are considered subtle energies that are located along the spinal column in various locations of the nervous system. There are many cultures, including Hindu, Tibetan, Hebrew, Chinese and Mayan that share the concept of a chakra model but nearly all cultures agree that the chakras are interrelated with a spiritual awakening or transformation. There is a specific purpose and theme to each chakra, and the chakras represent aspects of physical, emotional, mental and spiritual states.

Scientifically, chakras are capable of shifting energy from a lower vibration to a higher vibration. In the past twenty years, researchers of kinesiology have proved that chakras have a certain frequency reading. Certain healers, such as sound healers, can work with chakra energy to clear blocks and manipulate the energy fields.

Let me take you along a journey where you can visualize a small wheel, the size of a quarter strategically placed along the spinal column in your body.

Starting with Root Chakra at the front of the pubic bone, visualize a small circle the size of a quarter, totally stationery. It is a relic that has been there your whole life, but not ever activated. Now, give it the color red. Like using crayons in a coloring book, fill in this quarter sized circle, with a deep red hue. How can you get this circle to spin, or vibrate? This happens through manifestation and aligning with your values. By adding your own unique spark to your life and purpose, it acts like extracting positive vibrations to your circle or adding ingredients that are unique to you.

What is convenient about relating to a color, is that color is everywhere, and once you hold this awareness of relating the color with your energy center, it reminds you, that you are adding your positive feelings and thoughts to your chakra which helps keep it vibrant and alive within you. By focusing on this energy center with clear intention in mind, the Root Chakra will come to life through activation of the subtle energy systems that are in all of us.

These are an example of the types of elemental fuel

you can contribute to your chakra. Your chakra will start to turn very slowly at first, but as you add more and more positive energy, you will be able to *feel yourself heal* from within your chakra and really get focused in that special place. Consider this the beginning of your journey of learning how to resonate your root chakra, bringing special stories to your life, living with meaningfulness and purpose that makes you special. Before we begin using tools to create our mindfulness practice, let's dive deeper into the Root Chakra to get a good picture of what it is like and how you can *grow your glow*.

Root Chakra, also known as the Tribal Chakra, and in Hindu, Muladhara Chakra is the subtle energy center located at the base of the spine, at the first three vertebrae. It is also associated with the coccygeal nerve plexus. The Root chakra regulates your primal needs and serves as the foundation for physical survival. Root chakra can help you blend the awareness of foundation and the sense of belonging into your life through family or a circle of friends. Root chakra can help you to build stability in your life.

Honor your physical body by giving yourself proper nutrition and exercise, knowing that your body is the temple of your soul. Love yourself with compassion and nurture *you*, every day. Don't let the negative environmental energies take over your well being. Step up your game and vibrate positive energy throughout your day with red root chakra by firmly planting your feet onto the ground, knowing you are meant to be right where you are.

CHAPTER 2

GROUNDING

Try this: walk outside and take a look around. Feel the gentle breeze as it permeates your lungs, how it gives you energy deep within your body. Observe the trees and their vibrant, green personalities; some tall and majestic, others short and bushy. Feel the green grass under your feet, the softness, movement and resiliency of how it takes back its shape after your foot leaves that area. Inhale and exhale the air as it makes you aware of the energy and calmness it brings to your body.

Listen to the sounds of nature, the birds, the locust in the trees, the crickets, buzzing bees. This practice is known as Earthing, or grounding, and is yet another term for Root Chakra. The more you listen to Mother Nature and absorb the energies, the more aware you can become of your Root Chakra and the better your relationship with your own root energy to connect with nature. Nature is your friend and will help you enhance your root energy by magnetically attracting your glow internally.

To illustrate the glow of root chakra more clearly, I have been engrossed in Suzanne Simard's research who is a Professor of Forest Ecology at the University of British Columbia. She has conducted many experiments on the communications and intelligence of plants with one another through a root network under the forest floor. It turns out that trees communicate with each other via the mycorrhizal network, which is a network of fungi that link the roots of trees to one another and provide necessary nutrients to help each other grow and thrive (Jabr). Just think of yourself as a tree, with your own root system, sending your energy down this network through the Earth to help you grow your glow.

Root Chakra is aptly named since it is the base energy center where energy is manifested, just as a seed in the ground. Once the intention is created, the energy is activated at the base of the spine. Your roots begin to branch out, descending down each upper leg, through the knees, down into the calf area and finally to the soles of the feet. This is where your minor chakra points reinforce Root energy and become a catalyst to magnetically connect to the Earth energy, thereby causing a grounding effect.

It is no surprise that Earth is associated with Root chakra, which is a part of what makes this chakra even more special. Focusing on the root chakra every day can increase your awareness of Mother Earth and all living things upon it. It brings a sense of interconnectedness between you and your natural environment. All living creatures including plants on this planet are your sisters and brothers and you can expand on this, by feeling your intuitive energy connect with them. Listen to the birds and their songs, feel the grass, pay attention to the insects flying around you. They are there for support and will help you in culminating and owning your Root Energy. For example, Anthony William, known as the "Medical Medium" once said in his book by the same name, that the only place that "Spirit" would leave him alone and "stop talking to him" was when he visited the forest. (Williams p. 13) There is something magical and special about the community of trees, plants, animals, stones, water and sky that we have yet to appreciate. Just as Dr. Stephen Harrod

Buhner states in his book, *Sacred Plant Medicine: The Wisdom in Native American Herbalism*, we, as humans, can connect with plants through sensing and feeling and thus, communicating with plants intuitively. Using this concept can illustrate the relationship we already possess, which helps us connect directly, with Root Chakra Energy, through the ground and beneath.

Chapter 3

First Tool - Visualization

Your intention must be owning your root energy and letting it express itself through your senses. Feel and know your root energy, with strength and stability, as you ground your feet into the earth. You are distinctive and you were born to bring something special into this world. While grounding, this energy can flow both ways like a two-way highway from the Earth to the base chakra at the perineum or from the base chakra to the Earth.

This highway effect illustrates the meanings of Root Chakra: stability, foundation and strength. Pay attention whenever your sense of security and feelings of scattered energies form, ground yourself by visualizing your feet firmly planted into the ground, *growing your red glow.* This connection will help you tremendously any time of the day. Growing your red glow will keep you feeling confident and ready to take on the day wherever you may be. *Feel yourself heal* through grounded energy from the Earth, and get a sense of home and security in your body. Radiate red in your rainbow.

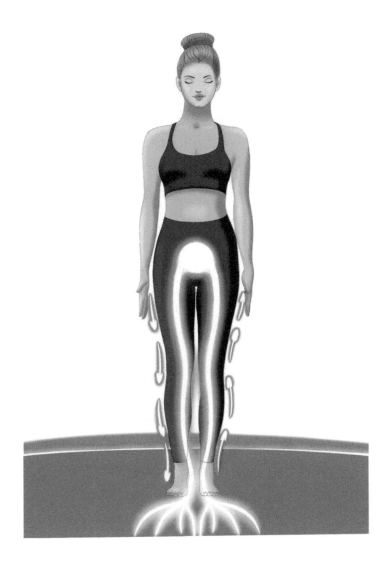

Congratulations, you have just witnessed using your first tool towards reaching your goal of a Mindfulness Practice with Root Chakra. Visualization is the first tool we will use throughout this book to activate Root Chakra. It is a powerful tool to help you realize your full potential using creative paths to start looking at new ways to keep you positive and alive with energy, yet calm and grounded.

Here is an example of a meditation you can try, to practice visualization.

Physical Seated Position: Sit on the ground with legs either crossed over each other or with the soles of the feet meeting in the middle (butterfly or cobbler pose). You may want your seat to be slightly higher than your legs. You can sit on a meditation pillow or a folded blanket. While seated, pull the flesh of your buttocks away from each other so that your sit bones are firmly planted on your support bolster, making sure your sit bones are tall and you are not tucked under.

You want to be in a neutral spine, where your spine feels tall and light and your abs and back are comfortably stable. Sitting, in this way, will keep you comfortable and able to stay seated for a long time. You can drape your arms on your knees, if you like, with palms facing up. If you are sitting in a chair, same goes for the positioning, keep the sit bones tall in your seat and stack your vertebrae in a comfortable, light, vertical position, keeping your shoulders away from your ears and relaxing the neck and surrounding areas.

Red Chakra Meditation Visualization Tool: Center yourself on red, warm, radiant sand, molding to your body, feeling your spine tall in your seat, feeling magnetically drawn to the ground. Now think of your sit bones, how each side is tall and stable. As you take your first deep breath on the inhale, and suspend your breath, visualize a beam of red, light energy at the base of your spine and, on the exhale, direct the energy downward into the Earth. Remember to fill the entire area with that warm, fiery energy. The area where your pubic bone, in the front of your body is located, straight through to your lower back area. Feel your connection to the ground.

Let's try it again: On the next inhale, feel the energy start to heat up. This swirling, red energy is how you grow your glow with Root Chakra. Now, exhale, feeling the energy as it descends from your perineum, down through your legs and out through your feet into the Earth. Activating your red, warm glow, will help you illuminate this energy outward and extend beyond your physical body as if a ring of energy surrounds you, starting right below your hips. Sit with this feeling of stability, comfort, security and belonging. Growing your glow with Root Energy is the beginning of your journey in stabilizing and bringing your tribal roots into your modern life.

CHAPTER 4

USING VISUALIZATION DURING MINDFUL EATING

Once you get a little more practice with visualizing the Red Root Chakra in a traditional meditation, we will work to open your mind into more action-oriented ways to use Red Root Chakra. One way to integrate mindfulness with Root Chakra is by practicing the art of mindful eating. This is a concept of Macrobiotics where you slow down the process of eating food by using your senses and concentrating your focus on the food and how it is eaten.

Once the senses of seeing, smelling, hearing, tasting and touching have all been activated about that food, you want to turn on your Root Chakra energy by adding this very important ingredient into your dish. The awareness of the Root energy really brings home the real attributes of the food and the nutrients within the food and creates a positive, healthy energy into your body. Especially if the food is energized with Root Chakra energy. For example, try eating a Red Delicious Apple to practice mindfulness and setting an intention.

The intention can be any one or two word phrase, or it can be a thought, but let's just say that the intention is Strong Support which reflects Root Chakra meaning. Start by observing the details of the apple, using your senses. While holding your red apple in your hands, use as many senses as possible. Examine its shiny, red skin, rich in soluble fiber, about 4 grams. Feel the smooth, round surface as your hand molds around it. Hear the crisp sound as you plunge your teeth into the flesh, tasting the cool, sweet juices and savoring the moment. As you swallow the apple bits, feel it travel down into your stomach. Feel the Vitamin C and antioxidants as they branch out to keep the walls of your small intestines strong. Interesting enough, the apple is "the ultimate colon cleanser" according to Anthony William, author of Medical Medium. Therefore, any red apple is a perfect example of tending to your Root Chakra Energy and keeping it healthy. This Red Delicious Apple is integrated into your strong, supportive body as Red Root Energy.

Mushroom energy is so Earthly and wonderful that it naturally culminates with Root Energy. Mushrooms are born in the ground and do not need light to grow like other edibles. But they are literally neighbors to roots of the ground making them rich with

Root Chakra energy. Knowing that mushrooms are grounding, due to their dark but thriving nature, the fascination of mushrooms coming from the ground, and able to be eaten, enhances the full effects of Root Chakra. The simple Button Mushroom, with its white and delicate surface, is easy to process into a salad raw or sauteed in some butter and seasoning which can really kick up the taste buds as soon as it hits your tongue.

Turning on your root energy grows your appreciation of the mushroom in all of its Earthly glory. Having the intention of root chakra activated, keeps your body in optimal condition while processing the superfood qualities of mushrooms. Mushrooms, any edible variety, have phytochemical compounds that inhibit tumor growth as well as contributing towards your increased immunity. Try some button or cremini mushrooms to help with grounding in your root chakra journey.

Another way to connect Root Chakra with food is through a recipe of your own. Remember, the energy that you put into creating your own recipe is enhancing your digestion in a creative way and doing it with Root Chakra Energy really builds your solid foundation. One of my favorite Smoothies is Muladhara Magic Smoothie infused with Root Chakra Energy. Here is the recipe for growing your own glow. Make it while your Root Chakra is activated, and *feel the heal* from within as your strong, grounding energy emits your red glow.

MULADHARA MAGIC SMOOTHIE

¼ cup of Strawberries
¼ cup of Raspberries
¼ of Pomegranate Seeds
5 Pineapple Chunks
½ cup of any Nut Milk
1 cup of Coconut Water
1 Scoop Vanilla Protein Powder
Essence of Root Chakra Energy

Pulse first four ingredients until pureed. Add remaining ingredients and pulse until smooth.

Feel free to create your own Root Chakra Recipes in any food category.

Chapter 5

Visualization during Physical Exercise

Another way to visualize with your root chakra awareness is through your exercise routine. Over the course of about 25 years, I have made the connection that chakra centers should be integrated into all types of exercises. Although this has been mapped out well in Yoga, the focus of the root chakra can enhance the power and endurance in grounding and lower body exercises.

Being mindful, while multitasking with exercise, can transition mind, body and spirit together energetically. The goal is to drop into that place of focus at the chakra center and use that awareness to integrate your mind into your activity. A good way to illustrate this, is by actively walking. Walking is one of the best ways to exercise because it is simple and you can start at any pace and for any length of time.

Try turning on your red root chakra by actively focusing on the red spinning energy at the base of your spine. Grow your glow by filling the entire lower back area, around your hips and through to the front of the pubic bone with red energy, really getting centered. Now, stream this energy by imagining it spreading down both legs, through the upper thighs, through the knees, down into the calves and glowing through the soles of the feet.

Plant your feet firmly on the ground, start your walk. You have now grounded yourself with root chakra energy, and with each step, you are fully connected with the energy of the earth. This bond of energy helps you feel stable and centered which creates strength and power with every step. Eventually, when you continue walking in this way, you can feel the energy exchange from the earth and in giving your energy to the Earth like a two-way highway effect. Your energy that you create from your root chakra is being exchanged with the earth's energy.

This can work as an outlet if you have negative energy that is building up. Just simply focus on that negative energy and flush it right out of your feet, then bring in new energy from the earth and replenish your body. Guess what? Your walking becomes more deliberate, your power and stability gets stronger, your mind becomes laser focused, your chakra is positively glowing. Living with intention and consistency can change your life.

This same visualization can work with any exercise related to the lower body. For example, the Power Squat.

- Stand with your feet a little wider than hip width apart.
- Feet straight ahead.
- Bend from the hip as if sitting in a chair, keeping the core into the spine, come to a 90 degree angle with your knees, butt back.
- Now activate your Root Chakra from the base of the spine
- Grow your Red Glow as you radiate this energy from the pubic bone in the front to the base of the spine in the back and fill this area with red energy.
- Once this area is filled, stream it down your legs into the earth. Feel this grounding energy and begin your squats.
- Draw up the stable energy through your legs as you squeeze your glutes at the top of the squat.

This is what it feels like to activate the Root Chakra while exercising. This movement brings the Body, Mind and Spirit into one cohesive action. This creates intention while performing a movement which is known to create positive energy fields.

Try working with this concept the next time you are working out. Start with something simple, like indoor or outdoor cycling. As you sit on the saddle, connect with your Root Chakra and visualize a red beam of light from your tailbone as it connects with the seat. Now, extend that red vertical beam through the seat and straight down into the ground. This focus will help you stay stable on the bike and build your confidence to continue with strong endurance.

As you get better at it, you can extend this energy down into your legs and out through your pedaling feet, energizing the entire bike and fusing your energy with the Earth. Exchanging energy in this way is one of the greatest visualizations to apply while exercising as it keeps your connection strong throughout the exercise and creates intention to go the extra mile.

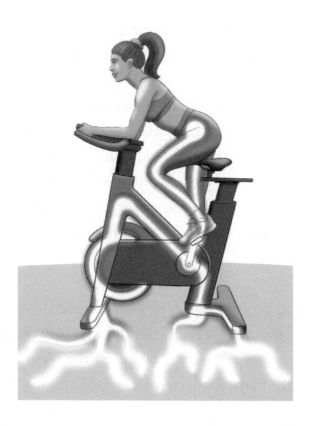

CHAPTER 6
TOOL #2 – SOUND WITH ROOT CHAKRA

While visualization is a great way to get started with your mindfulness practice, to go more in depth, you can add the use of sound to integrate Root Chakra into daily activities. Root Chakra energy is associated with the G Note according to Dr. Jeffrey Thompson, the founder of Scientific Sounds. Playing a G note on a guitar, piano or any instrument or just using a tuning app on your phone will get you familiarized with the note of root chakra.

Although the chakras have been in existence for many centuries, the musical notes that are associated with the chakras have only been recently discovered in the past thirty years. Dr. Jeffrey Thompson was one of the first to experiment with sound vibrations back in the 1990s when brain mapping equipment was released commercially. It is open for interpretation as to which note is associated with each chakra, but Dr. Thompson has proved through scientific experiments of the frequencies of the chakras and has matched up the information with mathematical formulas as to which note goes with which chakra.

However, according to Chakrakey.com, the musical notes can be intuitively interpreted and so, there are many versions of music note and chakra relationships. Intuitively, you can choose which note resonates better for you, but I will be following Dr. Thompson's chakra note interpretations. Once you become familiar with the G note, you can start to hum or sing the G note through your voice which can be used as a powerful healer.

This is a different way to focus on the G note and turn on your glowing red chakra energy. I find it a very powerful tool that will promote your own confidence and stability. Adding the visualization of your roots growing from the earth and feeling your energy flow from the ground will double the power in yourself. Try it and you will see the power that you can manifest. I experimented with this, when I first discovered that there were musical notes that were associated with each chakra.

I had recorded one note from my acoustic guitar, about 45 seconds in length and listened to it whenever time was available. After just a few weeks of doing this, I realized that since I was aware of the qualities of each chakra, I was increasing my development of those qualities. For instance, I wanted to see if I could increase my psychic abilities which are related to the Third Eye Chakra.

I started meditating to just the E note sound recorded from my guitar onto my phone. I would listen to the E note and visualize my third eye with a deep purple color. I would do this a few times a day for approximately three weeks. As a result, many psychic events were occurring that, at first, I was surprised. But after, a few more psychic thoughts, I was convinced that this was due to my little experiment and the fact that, I believe sound was activating these qualities energetically.

It would be little things, like I was thinking of this person and then they would call me. Little messages pop up all of the time now, which I just consider natural and part of my daily life. I encourage you to try this for yourself with a tuning app. The Root Chakra, for instance, resonates to the G note. Listen to the G note in the tuning app, and visualize your red energy radiating outward as you listen to the note. Next, add your visualization of tree roots glowing with red energy coming from the soles of your feet and *think* of your stability and physical foundation taking form within yourself.

An interesting theory presented by Chakrakey.com, is that our body is an instrument and the chakras are the strings. As we mindfully use these chakras with the musical notes, we achieve what is called harmonic resonance. I discovered this one day while I was drumming on my sacred drum and my acoustic guitar was nearby. I observed with great surprise that the A string started vibrating, and as I struck the drum harder, the string got louder and louder. I didn't know what this phenomena was at the time, but with some research, I was able to conclude that this is harmonic resonance.

The physical capability of vibrating a sound through the air and vibrating into another object. This energy can be translated into physical vibration, which can affect mental and spiritual positive mindfulness. Building on this concept, just as the energy is resonating into another instrument, be aware that vibrational energy from a tonal note can have a physical and mental effect in a positive way. I have witnessed, firsthand, that when I cause vibration on my tuning forks and place the base of them on my painful shoulder, the pain subsides for about a day and a half.

I can also get this effect with my Tibetan bowl. You will feel more relaxed and calm. Mentally, you will be more aware of being in the present moment, where nothing is bothering you. Now it's your turn to give it a try. Download a tuning app, I use Tuner- Pitched. You can also search Tuners to get an app that drags the note out a little more like on an electric guitar sound. It's a better way to hear the sound, if you have a note that lasts a long time, similar to a gong or Tibetan Bowl.

Find a quiet place to get comfortable, refer back to the physical seated position for more. Turn on your Root Chakra by *growing your glow.* Now chime the G note sound. Bring your attention to the G note, clearing your mind and either focusing silently or resonating the sound with your voice with an audible sound like a hum. Focus on your Root Chakra energy, feel your roots form through the bottom of your feet.

Feel planted into the ground, summon Earth energy to greet your body and feel the exchange of energy into your body. Feel the stability, the security, the strength, own your Root Energy. Gaze at something that is red, like a flower. Go deep with the G note sound, take yourself deeper with each chime and spread this energy from your perineum, down into your legs. Feel your red root glow and make your connection.

Eventually, as you practice, you will be able to add the feeling of your red glow from the root chakra.

Together, with the intent of going within root chakra and resonating the sound of G, you will notice Root chakra qualities start to surface every day. Your strength and stability will be more apparent. Your sense of security and confidence may change for the better.

You may venture out to do things you don't normally do. You may start to create a sanctuary at your home. Financial opportunities may open up for you. Your roots will become stronger with every step you take in your life.

CHAPTER 7

TOOL #3 – POSITIVE MINDSET USING ROOT CHAKRA ENERGY

I introduced visualization so you can begin to know and understand the feeling of your root chakra energy. I have helped you to enhance root energy with the use of sound. Next we'll cover the importance of a positive mindset to enhance your root chakra energy. These aren't ordinary affirmations, although all are great to use. These affirmations have been carefully crafted just for your Root Chakra Energy. These affirmations will help you to remember what root chakra means to you.

Always remember that you are a creative person and you can eagerly create your own Root Chakra Affirmations. Creating them can be fun and you can even make them into songs or poems. A good way to practice using these affirmations is to record them in your own powerful voice, on your phone, so you can listen to them anytime. This will amplify your positive energy while integrating Root Chakra energy affirmations into your daily practice. This is not limited to meditation. These recorded affirmations can be listened to at any time of the day for focus while at a desk job or just sitting while eating your meal or driving your car.

You are programming your mind to integrate Red Root Chakra while listening to these positive energy messages. Below are a few examples of positive mindset affirmations incorporating Root Chakra:

....

I draw positive vibrations from the Earth.

I am grounded.

I feel the magnetic connection to the Earth.

I am supported in my Truth.

My home is my sanctuary.

I feel a warm connection through my feet.

The Earth is inviting me to stand firmly.

I am safe and secure.

The earthly ground is my friend.

My feet are firmly planted.

My roots are strong and nurtured.

I connect with the ground.

My body stands tall on the ground.

I am a child of Mother Earth.

I feel the drumbeat of Mother Earth.

Warm red energy streams down my legs and
connects with the solid ground.

I love me.

I radiate love to others.

I illuminate love and kindness.

I believe in myself.

I am positive energy.

I am kind to my body.

I am grounded and centered.

I am rooted into the ground.

I am a red swirling glow of light.

I am strong Roots

I bind my energy with the Earth.

I feel vibrant.

I feel myself heal.

I grow my glow.

45

I can ground down.

I love from above.

I resonate with colored energy.

I crystalize positivity.

I feel content with my life.

I am at peace.

I am stress free and relaxed.

I feel expansion.

I draw positive energy into my soul.

I ignite grounding energy.

I am walking waves of light.

I draw positive vibrations from the Earth.

I exhale chatter.

G is for grounding.

Grounding energy is like a warm blanket.

Growing my red glow is soothing me.

My body feels supported in every way.

....

Another way to enhance these affirmations is to play the G note either right before or after you recite the affirmations. Or you can sing or chant the affirmation while you are playing the G note sound. Bringing the visualization of growing your red glow will enhance your experience even more. As soon as you bring your awareness to the Root Chakra, you are turning it on or activating it. You are changing your energy as soon as you start. Your creativity and your special qualities are coming out in a creative way.

CHAPTER 8

TOOL #4 - BREATHWORK WITH ROOT CHAKRA ENERGY

The last important pillar is using breathwork in your practice. Just as visualization can conveniently come with you anytime, breathwork is within your body and mind and so, you can activate this wherever you go. Your breath is a built-in mechanism for you to survive but how it is used in a mindful practice is magical and extraordinary. I will be introducing a few types of breathwork you can easily practice which are related to the Root Chakra. Your intention is to focus on Root, to grow your glow and enhance your practice with your breath.

I'd like you to try an exercise to get you centered with Root Chakra. Sit comfortably, sit bones vertical with a long spine, shoulders down away from the ears, with a neutral spine. Place your hands on your abdomen. Feel your breath, as it flows in and out and observe how your hands move when you do this. Now take a deep slow breath in so that the lungs are completely filled, and your tummy should be rising so that your hands are moving away from your spine. Hold the breath so that you can feel your heartbeat, now slowly let out the breath as your tummy comes in towards your spine.

This is the beginning of Breath of Fire. This practice

of quick, fiery breath activates your Root Chakra and starts to bring energy up the channels of the spine. It also has an added benefit of reducing stress, toning the abdominal wall and even improving digestion.

To begin this, you can start out very slowly, with your mouth open for inhales and exhales. Once you are familiar with it, you can start to do this faster and try it with your mouth closed, inhaling and exhaling through your nostrils. The force of the exhale will synchronize with your belly breath.

Another fun breath exercise to try is the 4-7-8 breath. This breath rules the nostrils of your nose so be sure to clear any obstructions, first. Sit comfortably, sit bones vertical, etc. Start by positioning your hand close to your nose. Using your mudra fingers, your middle finger and your thumb as your action fingers. These two fingers will be closing off your right and left nostrils as you do this breath. This breath synchronizes your hemispheres of your brain. Using your thumb alongside your nose, close off your right nostril, if you are right-handed, and use your middle finger to close off your left nostril. Just practice this back and forth before we start the breath.

Once you are comfortable with this motion, add the breath. Inhale one long breath through your left nostril on the count of four, pinch off both nostrils with both fingers and hold the breath for 7 counts. Exhale through the breath for eight counts through the right nostril. Now, inhale on the same right nostril, four counts, pinch off for seven counts and exhale, left nostril, eight counts. Keep doing this breath, starting out slowly. As you get the hang of it, you can speed the process but keep the count going 4-7-8. This breath is great to do when you lose focus of something or you are overwhelmed with anxiety. It keeps you calm and it centers your brain focus. You will be able to make better decisions at the spur of the moment.

Now put it together with growing your glow with Root Chakra. On your inhales, no matter the type of breath, think of drawing up your energy into your breath. This is not just any energy, it's your Root Energy. Inhale it through your feet up into your belly. Visualize the Root Energy moving up your roots, into your sit bone area and as you take deeper breaths, keep that strong root energy growing and glowing all the way up to your brain. Visualize your red glow as it migrates its way up and creates the two-way highway effect as you release that energy and flush it out through your feet back into the Earth. Growing your Glow from within and radiating it outward will change your energy field around you.

You are creating a new you, positively! It helps you function more efficiently and gracefully. Bringing your visualization into the practice with your red glow will enhance your laser focus to Root Chakra Energy. You can use this practice anywhere. While you are at the office, on the road, it is a breath that can reprogram your brain to center and create focus and calmness in about 30 seconds. It is the antidote to anxiety, boredom, confusion, sadness or a host of any negative feelings that may try to creep in.

Your body is a unique being with infinite possibilities and it is designed just for you. It has these built-in, customized features that you may not be aware of. Your own body can get yourself out of sticky situations. If you feel overwhelmed, practice breathwork. It will change you positively. It brings confidence, it lifts your spirits, it keeps you calm and it is always with you.

CHAPTER 9

ENHANCEMENTS INTEGRATED WITH ROOT CHAKRA ENERGY

Using visualization, sound, affirmation and breath-work coupled with Root Chakra Energy brings new life to your mindfulness practice. There are always embellishments that can be used to amplify these pillars. For instance, using your empath sense to feel

Root Chakra Energy is always a good way to amplify your visualization practice. Not only are you visualizing your red energy but you can feel the warmth or even hotness of the energy sitting at the base of your spine.

In some of you, this may be easier to do then visualizing, so feel free to play around with it. With sound, there are several ways to get creative with the G note Root Energy. One way is to use tuning forks. You can buy a tuning fork that is tuned to the G note which is also known as 384 hz. Strike the tuning fork on a hard rubber surface to make the fork ring and you can place the base of the stem of the fork directly to your pubic bone or an area near your Root Chakra to amplify the energy and bring your chakra to life.

Focus on the sound of the fork and let your glow grow with red chakra energy. Again, you can play with whatever ingredients you want to add to your recipe of your mindfulness practice. You can add the grounding technique and visualization to get even more focused. Another great way to amplify is by using crystals or stones. There are many varieties of crystals that can be used with Root Chakra Energy.

Most of these crystals are either red, brown, grey or black. Some types of stones associated with Root Chakra are: Carnelian, Agate, Obsidian, Hematite, Tiger's Eye, Ruby, Garnet or Red Coral. There are different frequencies that amplify Root Chakra that will change your energy or clear blocked energy. Feel free to play around with these enhancements to get the full effect of focusing on your practice with Root Chakra.

I like to hold the stones in my hands while practicing breathwork or you can wear them on a necklace or in your pocket. Knowing that you have these stones near you are helping to enhance your root chakra energy. By now, you should be able to recognize the Root Chakra location in your body, "turn on" your root chakra energy by *growing your glow* and using the four tools to help build on your Root Chakra practice.

It is up to you on how you want to mix it up during your day. Eventually, you will be able to relate anything red that you see during your day with Root Chakra Energy such as a Stop sign on the street or a red apple, or a red leaf on a tree. This is how you can keep your energy engaged all day long. You'll start associating red with grounding, security and power and even start to recite some of your affirmations.

This all turns on your chakra energy and it keeps you focused every time. It will come to your rescue in time of need. It will keep you neutral, knowing you are ok and you can handle whatever is thrown at you. Just keep your feet firmly on the ground and know that you can handle anything with Root Chakra Energy.

For example, I recently had an accident where I broke my fibula in my left leg. When that happened,

I was by myself and I immediately started to feel my roots grow and glow into the Earth. I was able to calmly call 911 Emergency and get to the hospital by myself without even raising my blood pressure. Later, while at the hospital, my pain was minimal. After getting home with all of the necessary equipment, I was able to rest, re-center with Root Chakra Energy and start to heal my bone with my own special root energy. With my own Medicine bag of Visualization, Sound, Affirmations and Breathwork, I was able to heal my fibula sooner than expected. I visualized my glowing, red energy, naturally coming from my Root Chakra, visualizing my roots streaming down my leg and actually mending my bone. At the same time, I was synchronizing the sound of the Tibetan Bowl with my breath and flushing the negative energy of my broken bone out through my minor root chakras in my feet. Once this was done, I recited one of my affirmations, Growing My Red Glow Is Soothing Me. Enhance your healing with Root Chakra Energy and receive the messages as they come. It will surprise you.

Knowing that we have this amazing energy rooted into our self, and that we can draw upon it whenever necessary, is a true gift. Growing our glow from within, and radiating it outward, brings our life more vitality and keeps our spark positive. Just as the roots from under the magnificent tree brings forth nutrients to the tree above ground, so the root energy brings forth messages to you and helps you to strive towards your better self. Roots always bring you to what you know and love. They are the network that helps you to know yourself more completely. Your Root Energy takes you within your deepest being and keeps you firmly planted to take on the challenges that come your way. Knowing how to apply it in your everyday life just takes a little practice, but it will change your perception of your world and how you live it.

BIBLIOGRAPHY

Johari, Harish. *Chakras Energy Centers of Transformation.* Destiny Books, 2000, pp. 71-94.

William, Anthony. *Medical Medium – Life Changing Foods.* Hay House, Inc. 2016, pp. 48-49, 236-237.

William, Anthony. *Medical Medium.* Hay House, Inc. 2015, p. 13.

Jabr, Ferris. "The Social Life of Forests." 02 Dec 2020 www.NYTimes.com/interactive/2020/12/02/magazine/tree-communciation-mycorrhiza.html

Ireton, Rick. "Chakra Frequencies and Correlations." 2017 www.chakrakey.com/chakra-frequencies-and-correlations-2/

Buhner, Stephen Harrod. *Sacred Plant Medicine: The Wisdom in Native American Herbalism.* Bear and Company, November 2005.

Fuhrman, Joel. *Super Immunity: The Essential Nutrition Guide for Boosting Your Body's Defenses to Live Longer, Stronger and Disease Free.* HarperOne, 2011, Chapter 3 Super Foods for Super Immunity – Life Saving Mushrooms.

"The Chakras." YouTube, uploaded by Dr. Jeffrey Thompson, 28 June 2020.

"The Chakras Part 2." YouTube, uploaded by Dr. Jeffrey Thompson, 5 July 2020.

Dale,Cyndi. *The Subtle Body An Enclyclopedia of Your Energetic Anatomy.* Sounds True: Boulder, Colorado, 2009.

Rosenthal, Joshua. *Integrative Nutrition A Whole-Life Approach to Health and Happiness.* Integrative Nutrition Inc.: New York, 2018.

BIOGRAPHY

Lisa Reda, with years of study in yoga, and as a fitness instructor, has been able to combine the mind/body/spirit balance into her clients' daily lives as an Integrative Health Coach. She has been highly successful in coaching clients in bringing awareness to themselves, realizing their full potential and reducing stressful scenarios. She is also a specialist in Sleep Health Coaching. Lisa enjoys learning guitar, practicing belly dancing, studying herbalism and plant spirit medicine, and bike riding. If you would like to make some lifestyle changes, please go to www.Nutritionintuition.help for more information. She currently resides in Wappinger Falls, NY with her husband and three daughters.

Acknowledgments

To the Institute for Integrative Nutrition and founder, Joshua Rosenthal for inspiring me to "Think Big" and "create a ripple effect that transforms the world".

To Rick Gabrielly for helping me bring this book into reality with his expertise in all facets of book creation.

To Clare Davidson, for her amazing art design, layout and professionalism.

Special thanks to Eva Vera for providing interior sketches that conveyed my message perfectly.

Thank you to Tracey Gayle, my accountability coach. I couldn't have even started without you. Having support while on a book adventure makes all the difference.

Thank you to Carmela Contento, my "Aunt Millie" for being on the same high vibration and giving me just the right information, in divine and perfect timing. We are telepathically connected.

I am extremely grateful to my husband, Vincent, who has patiently and gracefully encouraged me to write this book. His continuing support is a gift to me every day.

Thank you, Amy Rodriguez, for encouraging me to

become a Health Coach. I didn't even know what a Health Coach was, until we had a conversation about it.

Made in the USA
Columbia, SC
30 June 2021

41232319R00049